IT'S TIME TO EAT PISTACHIOS

It's Time to Eat PISTACHIOS

Walter the Educator

Silent King Books
A WhichHead Entertainment Imprint

Copyright © 2024 by Walter the Educator

All rights reserved. No part of this book may be reproduced in any manner whatsoever without written per- mission except in the case of brief quotations embodied in critical articles and reviews.

First Printing, 2024

Disclaimer

This book is a literary work; the story is not about specific persons, locations, situations, and/or circumstances unless mentioned in a historical context. Any resemblance to real persons, locations, situations, and/or circumstances is coincidental. This book is for entertainment and informational purposes only. The author and publisher offer this information without warranties expressed or implied. No matter the grounds, neither the author nor the publisher will be accountable for any losses, injuries, or other damages caused by the reader's use of this book. The use of this book acknowledges an understanding and acceptance of this disclaimer.

It's Time to Eat PISTACHIOS is a collectible early learning book by Walter the Educator suitable for all ages belonging to Walter the Educator's Time to Eat Book Series. Collect more books at WaltertheEducator.com

USE THE EXTRA SPACE TO TAKE NOTES AND DOCUMENT YOUR MEMORIES

PISTACHIOS

Crunchy, green, and oh so sweet,

It's Time to Eat
Pistachios

It's time to eat pistachios, a special treat!

In little shells, they like to hide,

But crack them open, there's joy inside!

One by one, let's give them a try,

They're tasty snacks, and here's why:

They're fun to peel, they're good for you,

And every bite feels fresh and new!

Pile them high upon your plate,

These tiny treasures sure taste great!

A pinch of salt, or plain is fine,

Pistachios shine every time!

A snack for morning, noon, or night,

They're always just the perfect bite.

Take your time, don't eat too fast,

The fun in cracking makes them last!

It's Time to Eat
Pistachios

Green as grass and creamy, too,

Pistachios bring a happy hue.

Pop them in, and you will see,

How yummy healthy snacks can be!

Tiny shells go "snap" and "crack,"

With every bite, you'll want them back.

In your pocket, take a few,

A perfect snack for things you do!

Picnic time or on the go,

Pistachios steal the snack-time show.

They make you smile, they're so much fun,

A happy treat for everyone!

So grab a bowl, let's have a feast,

Of pistachios, the snack-time beast!

Crunch and munch, then have some more,

It's Time to Eat
Pistachios

Until the shells pile on the floor!

When snack time's done, and we're all through,

Let's clean up shells, just me and you.

We'll save the rest for another day,

Pistachios make the fun stay!

So now you know, it's oh so neat,

Why it's time to eat pistachios, sweet!

A tasty treat for all to share,

It's Time to Eat Pistachios

Pistachios show how much we care!

ABOUT THE CREATOR

Walter the Educator is one of the pseudonyms for Walter Anderson. Formally educated in Chemistry, Business, and Education, he is an educator, an author, a diverse entrepreneur, and he is the son of a disabled war veteran. "Walter the Educator" shares his time between educating and creating. He holds interests and owns several creative projects that entertain, enlighten, enhance, and educate, hoping to inspire and motivate you. Follow, find new works, and stay up to date with Walter the Educator™

at WaltertheEducator.com

www.ingramcontent.com/pod-product-compliance
Lightning Source LLC
LaVergne TN
LVHW052014060526
838201LV00059B/4025